Hard To Be a Hero

Hard To Be a Hero

Poems by

Alec Solomita

Cover design by Shay Culligan
Cover image by Andres Molina on Unsplash

ISBN: 978-1-63980-105-3

Kelsay Books
502 South 1040 East, A-119
American Fork, Utah 84003
Kelsaybooks.com

For Vincent and Nadia
in memory

Acknowledgments

Thanks to the editors of the publications in which these poems first appeared, sometimes in a slightly different form and sometimes differently titled.

The Galway Review: "Closing In On Seventy," "Summer," "Nightlife," "Dancer," "There Are Mysteries," "Morality Tale," "The Way We Live Now," "Directive," "Missing You Again," "Last Evening," "Like Swallows Singing," "Nuance"

The Blue Nib: "All-Star"

Algebra of Owls: "Hard To Be a Hero," "The Sisters," "I'm Walking Home"

The Lake: "Handy Man"

Silver Birch Press: "High Tide"

MockingHeart Review: "Tommy," "Elvenoy"

Noctua Review: "The Time We Almost Got Our Heads Mashed In"

Litbreak: "Debby"

Truck: "Jurisprudence," "Upstate"

Turk's Head Review: "Dystopia," "Access"

Rat's Ass Review: "*Le Vrai Roi,*" "Crucifixion," "Black Ops"

Poetry Circle: "Invitation"

Cherry House Press: "Seasonal"

Streetlight: "Snowstorm"

Poetry Box: "I've Walked Down"

Brighten Sea Anthology: "Familiar"

Far Away Places: "Raptor" (also in chapbook *Do Not Forsake Me*)

Anti-Heroin Chic: "Rain Dove," "After the Funeral," "Keeping Busy"

The New Criterion: "Echolocation"

Do Not Forsake Me: "Missing"

Panoplyzine: "We Were Sitting by the River"

Eclectica: "Crazy For You"

Lothlórien Poetry Journal: "The Dell," "Self-Help"

I am grateful to all those who, one way or another, were a part of this book. My thanks to Mary Beth Hines, Emily Axelrod, and E. Scott Slater for their thoughtful, generous reading and editing of the manuscript in its different stages; I am grateful as well to Susan Tepper, Leah Xue, Tom Daley, John Canaday, Frannie Lindsay, and Marcus Strider Jones, for their discerning eyes, ears, and moral support. And special thanks to my great teacher, Katia Kapovich.

Contents

III

IV

V

I

Closing In On Seventy

Ten years old on a breezy day
in March of '63, a boy climbing
a long slant of lawn
paused to scan the sky

and a sudden serenity
descended upon him,
or perhaps rose from
the moist earth. He stood

as still as the beech beside him
while fall's dead leaves, released from
old snow, swirled 'round his shoes.

As I close in on seventy,
the child comes with me,
taking my hand as a child will.

All-Star

We shinnied up the slender, smooth-barked,
young beech, pulled ourselves onto
the garage roof, and sat on the canted edge
until the courage came to push off,
me and my brother Sal. I was older
and full to the brim, taking the leap
with something like savoir faire
while Sal sat sometimes for hours
as the sun ambled across the summer sky,
his arms 'round his bare knees, marshaling
some deeply embedded mystery before letting go.
When the moment came, he leapt
like a dancer into the dime-bright air,
springing from cloud to cloud to
billowy cloud until all I could see
were the soles of his white Converse All-Stars.

Hard To Be a Hero

For a small boy it's hard to be a hero,
something you generally have to arrange
for yourself by, say, starting a fire
in the deserted lot behind your house,
littered with dry stalks of chicory,
volunteer honeysuckle, a ruptured mattress.
And when the slow smoke finally flames,
running to your mother bent over her
ironing board to sound the alarm, then
running back while she's on the phone
to watch the engines roll in and hear
the sirens call.

Handy Man

The trees in the sloped yard cringe
as Vince starts to barbecue again.
I always wanted a dad with a neat
workroom in the basement, tools
hanging in coherent rows. He pours
out the charcoal into the black circle.
The rumble is pleasing; I light a cigarette
way up on the porch, out of harm's way.
"That's enough!" cries my mother
as flight patterns of lighter fluid send
streaks of fire 'round the bare legs of my
little sister who knocks over the table
covered with raw hamburger and hot dogs.
The only thing worse is watching him
try to set up the Christmas tree.

The Sisters

Mother Superior perches on a bough
above the snow, her eyes everywhere.

Sister Francesca, cranky as an old wife,
reads John Greenleaf Whittier
to a roomful of inkwells.

The mortal remains of Sister Marie Perpetua
disperse in St. Patrick's Cemetery
while her soul slow-dances with the Lord.

High Tide

When the tide was high in Magnolia
I took to the sea,
eyeing the swell of the forming waves
with a child's expertise,
gauging the breaks,
pumping up the foaming crest,
to surrender my small, tumbling body,
as they say in AA,
to a higher power.

Summer

I remember my patience as a boy
watching the sun slide behind
a cloud and then, for as long
as it took, following the dim
moonlike disc idle its way
to the other side until it began
its unhurried blinding exit,
turning the world back to bright.
And I remember the time I turned
from the sky to be surprised by you
tiptoeing behind as you put your
thumb on the nozzle of the hose,
grinning your evil dazzling grin.

Tommy

Dark things happen in basements,
dusty bulbs dangling,
tang of dirt and wood.
"When he sings in the choir," my mother,
whose footsteps creak above us,
says about Tommy, "he looks like an angel."
Tommy bends over Charlie and her kittens,
his hair blue-black like Archie's Veronica,
face creamy, unblemished Irish.
My breath hitches when he
gently tosses the kitten, catches it,
tosses it again not so gently,
its sprawly, tiny body rising closer to
the creaking ceiling. My insides
run like blood, a liquid turn, soldier's joy.
The final toss is a fling into the rafters,
the small thump, the limp rebound,
Tommy's sated smile, my crooked one.
He lifts it by the tail and places it pianissimo
among its live, nuzzling siblings.

Weird Science

"Can you believe this heat? You can fry an egg on the sidewalk."

And how much time did we waste,
if waste time one can do at eight,
trying to fry an egg on the driveway
on those blazing days that reached
the nineties and, once or twice, beyond?

Kneeling on swelling black asphalt
in crinkled blue jeans, crouching in yellow
sun dresses with red hearts, carefully
cracking the egg and watching it, and
with what patience, as it runs and lies still.

Wind Chill

Man oh man. Ain't been this cold
since I was fifteen and Patty Walsh
said she wouldn't go out with me,
and I went to see the movie
Tom Jones and four rows ahead
was Patty with Joey Young's
arm around her.

Elvenoy

At Mass, my blood bumped when I held
the golden plate under Elvenoy's double chin,
kneeling in her ruffled dress, stretching out
her bubbly, pink tongue, her brown eyes raised
to heaven as Our Lord melted away.

"Wanna show ya somethin'" she said one day,
her shy head lowered, her dark eyes rolling
toward the dark garage, its interior webbed with light,
where she put her tongue in my mouth and raised
her ruffled dress.

The Time We Almost Got Our Heads Mashed In

I thought it was the end,
me and my cousin, just boys
thumbing home at three in the a.m.
tired and happy from doing nothing
all night, hanging with the gang
drinking Budweiser and Schlitz,
letting the girls sit on our jackets
to watch dense clouds of bats
swirl from tree to dark tree
against a periwinkle sky
when a car brakes and backs up
and a wiffle-headed teen leans out
a side-window and says, "There's
room." Just barely I think as David
squeezes next to three football fucks
in the back and me next to the two
in front. The driver clears his throat
and on a sudden wing of clarity,
I think, "Oh, shit, this is the end."
"So, here's the story, cats," he begins
in a chatty tone ("Cats?" I think),
"If you don't cough up some bread,
we're gonna mash your heads in."
Right away I begin to beg.
But badly; I was shy, a whelp
of a boy, so David steps in slick
and calm, tells them our mom's sick
our dad's a cop and our older
brother's in the Marines and how we
got no bread at all, hardly a dime
between us. In just moments, following
some sort of telepathic huddle,

the bipeds choose to let us go with a final
warning, a simple "We'll pop you if
we see you again." The Buick stops
and they shove us out onto Storrow Drive.
("Pop?") I think, all gladness and bruises.
"Pop?" I say to David, "Cats?" he says back
and we take off down the black highway,
shaking with laughter as we run for our lives.

Debby

I can remember still
the slope of the green dell,
the blade of grass between Dave's teeth
while we watched Debby and her shifting hips
stroll toward us, an impish, tilted grin
kindling her pale face as she navigated the narrow lane.
After we told our tales and smoked our smokes
and after I recalled her as a tumbling child:
(even then she'd surprise me with secret pokes
in secret places. Oh, she was brimful of need
even at eleven, that buoyant, neglected girl),

we three sat on the sloping hill, our hands
behind us on the damp grass, our souls expanding,
as the bluing sky seemed to expand, with love
for Deb, for David, for me, for the dark that fell from above.

Nightlife

In all my dreams I'm young again,
pale green as the underside of leaves
in my climbing tree in the backyard.

II

Dancer

A young woman dances alone
to "Fire on the Mountain"
in the Brewers' Bar in Brattleboro.
In her floor-skimming dress
and waist-length hair,
she lifts her hands over her head
and moves in little half-circles
on the yeasty floor, humming loud
enough to herself so you hear her
over the music, and when she's done,
the audience rises spontaneously
to its feet and bursts into tears.

Jurisprudence

Her charm utterly disarmed the prosecution
and from then on all was effervescence.
The judge donned a white tasseled robe
and called for a short recess, which was
held in the school yard with many
of the jury playing dodgeball with
the well-put-together and droll stenographer.
Stenography is not as easy as it appears,
and one of the more interesting evidentiary
plums plucked from long fluorescent
night classes is that fingernails
grow in the coffin and so does hair.
That being said, after recess came snack-time—
animal cookies carrying attaché cases.

Upstate

The apes play hide and seek in the woods.
Jenny complains bitterly, her morning walks
ruined by cries of "I see you," and "You're It!"
Meanwhile, barn owls roost in the barn,
keeping yellow eyes out for red foxes.
Every single person at the grange voted but
there was no majority. Too many
persuasive arguments from both sides.
"They frighten the children."
"Think of the tourist potential."
The folks congregate on the steps, perplexed.
When faced with a conundrum, the farmer pauses.
The origin of the apes was unclear but they all knew that
thousands of cranes would return in the spring.

There are Mysteries

There are mysteries left to confound us:
The cohomology classes of Hodge
The non trivial zeroes of Riemann
The lubricious clergyman's dodge
Why people go rock climbin'
The Yang-Mills mass gap
The smoothness of Navier-Stokes
People who buy socks at the Gap
Those who say "just folks"
The conjecture of Swinnerton-Dyer and Birch
The orientation of Peter Pan
How Scarlet Johansson could be left in the lurch
Why some still say, "I'm going to the can"
O, there are mysteries left to confound us.

Morality Tale

Virtue crawls through his beard like
lice, an apt accessory to the branches
and banana peels in his composting biz.
My man! Reducing methane emissions

is just one sign of his beneficence.
Was a time we'd call him a know-it-all;
now we just eye him biking by, his
bins filled with rot, his smile a smirk.

I tend to hold a grudge till the eagle grins:
Dropped a buck once to an old teeter on a grate
and Mr. Man says, "You shouldn't give them
money. There are better ways to give.

He'll just spend it on booze." "Just?"
I said. Stopped at the corner packie,
procured a pint, sat down on the sidewalk
by my new dawg and shot the shit till dawn.

Dystopia

The summer bike path, dapple and green.
A biker frightens an ancient couple,
not with speed but a warning
(*'On your left!'*). Boys of prey
saunter indolently, waiting for dark.
Vaguely bovine young women
herd daily-abandoned four-year-olds
by the dozen—same green shirts, same
chubby knees, tied together with
ribbon, bewildered, blinking in the
sunny spaces between the big leaves.
And, O! the runners: Flushed dismal
Lolitas, nether cheeks exposed in shorts
labeled 'Pink.' Starving gray Furies
grimly huffing into the foul air.
And the dogs. O, the dogs! Many
tiny, these days, and white. And their
walkers, each with his own plastic bag.

Better This Than That

As the knobby spine of night softens into
day, I lie in bed dream-scoured and scared,
but nightmares or not, I want to get back to sleep.
I prefer fantastic fear to quotidian despair.
I'll take the weird dream about the British
barrister with the erect carriage, and the bent
erection, the left eye with its white film
and the right one that twirls like a pinwheel.

Le Vrai Roi

No, I don't want Vicodin, Oxycontin
or fentanyl—the dauphin and his boys.
Opiates! What a weak word!
Pills for panty-waists!
I want *le vrai roi*.

I want a den as dark as sleep,
bunk beds and ancient ministrations,
great mysteries just out of reach of my languid fingers
waxing and waning in the bowls of clay pipes.

How the *Lumières* Adore It

How the *lumières* adore it
When one of their own slings shit
At the mercantile herd.

Rabelais wrote *menus:*
To start, "fine turds" and "shitlets"
Followed by "collard bullfarts"
And for dessert, well, let's skip dessert.

Celine, as he matured,
Relished a good scat joke
Almost as much, "Then he pokes
Around his underpants, sticks
His finger in his butt…"

And Jarry, he's the king of them all,
Smearing excrement on doorknobs
To fool those *imbéciles* with day jobs,
The smug and costive bourgeoisie.

Moi? J'aime la bourgeoisie.
J'adore my neighbor who sweeps
The sidewalk fronting his yard.
God Bless Mrs. Ogmore-Pritchard!
Vive Marcel Pagnol!

Adult Education

A room full of was,
dozing while teacher finds
slides of Copley and West

on his laptop. The room's
weak light slips away
with a sigh of relief.
The door opens and shuts

by itself. A woman coughs
until her specs fall on the table.
At least Copley's odd shark has
a good shot at a satisfying snack.

Perseveration

Watch the bad marriage that dawdles—
presumptive adults unable to toddle
off to the exit, though both shrinks say
you won't "grow" until you break away.

Do the rewards simply outweigh grievances?
His appalling parents trumped by their distance,
her fault-finding aced out by ardor in the dark,
his unearthly poise when she listens to P!nk,

shared fondness for green tea and medical dope,
foodism, and the lingering hope
he'll stop whining, and she'll stop baiting,
that her friends won't mock and he'll stop hating

the joke she tells every day: "that train has sailed."
A glance at the scales, and others see a love that's failed.
But it's been so long and both adore the big city,
and as they say, nothing propinks like propinquity.

The Way We Live Now

I binge the old-fashioned way
so at about eight in the evening
I'm feeling kind of carefree
and want a chat with a fellow imbiber.
But everyone is binge-watchers these days,
and before they turn on *Vera* or *The Crown*
or that old bore Father Brown,
what do they do? You know because
you do it, too. They turn off their phones!
And I'm left alone with a drink in my hand.
It's the new "we're having dinner,"
where politely answering a call is verboten.
I remember when the phone was in the kitchen
and my long-gone ma was in the living room
watching *Queen For a Day* or *Doctor Kildare*.
When she heard the ring she hauled herself
without protest, support hose and all,
out of her comfy armchair to answer the call.

III

Humid

The clouds are big with sleeping thunder.
Air sits on the skin. Gleaming children
shoot layups in the drive, and through
the window I feel the slap of the ball
on asphalt, the shouts of the kids
almost drenched by the time they reach me.

Invitation

The sea looks like it wants an RSVP.
Now that it's night, I feel like accepting.
Now that it's night and the fat man
with the Bruins cap who stood waist deep
from low tide to high cupping water over
his blistered paps is gone, along with
the moat-mad castle builders and their
Romance-addled mums. And those
girls, those girls, in threes and fours,
flatfooted and quick on firm sand,
shaped like all desire, now that they are gone,
I muscle through the swelling brine
up to my shoulders, only to ease onto my back
and, held up by the sinewy dark, decline.

Seasonal

Here they are the brief, dark days,
the hard ground, the savage wind
stabbing bent, quilted pedestrians.
People too old to run chase buses like dogs

or sit at windows, dreaming of wood stoves,
fireplaces, and the flickering dead,
or lie clothed in their beds as the day
ebbs and evening dresses the trees

in traditional black. Or they recall old Eddie
the ancient soda jerk on children's summer
weekends. Vanilla milkshake. Red rotating stools.
Shaded suburban porches dark as the empty schools.

The bus doesn't stop. The old man slips
and recovers in graceless, teetering slapstick,
then quickly looks around, more afraid of
ridicule than the last broken hip.

Snowstorm

Odd. As it lands, the snow ticks.
I lean on the shovel
to calm my old heart.
It's wet snow and it sticks

to everything—the porch, the railing,
like thick lines of cocaine,
which also at this point, would
doubtless get my old heart skirring.

I hear echoes of my widowed
dad's anxious fingernails in the ticking of the snow.
Last time I saw him, snow fell silent and steady
down a dark blue sky, onto snowed-

in windows, white trees, white streets.
His wife wasn't in the world anymore.
His mourning would never end,
his tears as sudden as the splash of sleet

shooting up from the one passing car
on this silent night, too white, too lovely
even to curse at the driver
hunched over his wheel trying to steer.

I Love the Spring

'And that sweet man, John Clare'

I love the spring,
lilac charming the air,
buds nippling in the faithless warmth,
forsythia igniting overnight.
I love the last of the ragged snow
slipping filthy into storm sewers,
old people peeking out from
under winter's burrows.
I love the not quite nameable
vapors floating from the loosened
belt of ice, moist earth gasping,
exhaling a jolt of childhood.

The Dell

Out of the talk and laughter of the little house,
its wine and sopressata and local brew,
I stepped through the porch, pulled the door to,
and the silence of the night served to rouse
me more than all the clamor: John had passed,
I'd just been told by a fool I'd known for fifty years.
I stood and watched a high wind chase as if in fear
some tattered clouds across the dark sky, when at last

I understood. "Passed?" I'd thought, what? the bar?
His chemistry test, leaning over the Bunsen's blaze
next to Deb Stein with her bony knees and cross-eyed gaze?
But the verb was intransitive, I saw, blinking at a blinking star.
John's passing had no object, and I almost fell:
all those times he'd tackle us laughing in the green dell.

I've Walked Down

I've walked down this uneven brick sidewalk
in bright December, in springtime splendor,
in evening dress, unshaven, unshorn, balding
and drunk, slick and slim, smooth and sober,
in t-shirts and cargo shorts on closing summer nights.

I walked up a similar sidewalk, swollen
reddish brick, the heart of old Boston,
where I first smoked grass forty-eight
years ago in a tiny apartment with a skinny
blonde who assured me that one of these times
I would feel it. And she was right. I feel it now,
an old man, high as a kite (the bird, not the toy)
looking down on my own life, my only prey.

Directive

My dear young friend,
there's a familiar old saw
you might find useful.
I keep it in the shed.
Feel free to borrow it
to cut a walking stick
with a nice knob for its head
and a good barky grip.

When the prattling world
and its current cant
starts to rattle your brain,
take it for a stroll
off the pious path
into the hushing trees
where the sounds are few
and profess nothing.

IV

Crazy For You

Listen to this!
When I see you
I want to kiss
your mouth
and hold your hands,

listen to all your plans
slip through your lips,
and all the laments—
your dad, your mom, your heavy sis,

listen to you hiss
"I'm crazy for you,"
when whiskey sipped from nips
unhooks your hips.

Grotto

What's as wistful and more precious
than this young woman
with her shorn bangs and raised
arm, pressing her nipples so they
flatten gently and breathtakingly
against the shower glass, her figure
and face smudged by reflections,
her knowing pose, her hips curved
in reverence to Eros, her camera-wise eyes
and passive face full of history
and the determination to be desired?

Crucifixion

When she bends over, I want to cross her like a bridge,
linger as I pass over her curled feet, over her flattened calves,
freckled manna, nibble the flake-like, honeyed flesh.
Ascend solemnly the call and response of her thighs,
running my hand between like the strains of an organ,
then heavenward toward her buttocks, a psalm of David
cleft by his sorrow over Absalom. And there I rest
in their lament and beauty, and my body answers.
A sigh long and lovely as the Song of Solomon escapes
her mouth. She turns to me, eyes green as perfidy,
lips thick, swollen lies until they rise in a smile
simple and sunny as a proverb. I inch up her back
entering her like a rich man through a needle's narrow eye.
Her arms spread out like crossbars, where I rest my own.

If Your Breaths Were Angels

If your breaths were angels
and your tongue was sweet
and your lips were brown and full
I would be complete.

If your legs were dark and long
and your breasts did sway
and your center savory,
I could die today.

Let me breathe your breath my dear,
let me lick your tongue.
Let me kiss your full brown mouth,
let me rest among

your raspy middle curls,
your swelling nether lips,
my face gently rocking
in your rocking hips.

Black Ops

I thought I had a chance
with you, but you up and
moved—to St. Louis
for Jesus' sake! That,
as they used to say in
St. Louis, is "a fer piece"
from Beantown, which
no one says here.

You really are something,
downing dirty martinis
like the soldier you are,
bitching about gun laws,
what a dick your ex was.
Listening when I talked,
I mean, seriously.

And how many soldiers
look like you? How many?
So gifted in the bust!
So flushed and redhaired!
And we go out for drinks
Twice. No—three times. Then you
slip off to St. Louie Louie.

And who, as it turns out,
is *in* St Louis?
A boyfriend, a Ranger.
I don't know…
I knew basic training
was a bitch, but I don't know
whether to go blind
or wind my watch.

Nuance

I said I'm falling in love with you.
You said unh so quietly I might not have heard
that softest grunt of long yearning.
Right away I thought maybe I should have said,
I think I'm falling in love with you

or I want you. I want you so bad.
But that's the thing, I thought,
as you put your fingertips to your temples
and looked up. I did want you so bad
so I said I'm falling in love with you.

Missing You Again

Thought I saw you on the street.
They say it happens with the deceased:
your mother maybe or your long gone da,
or our aunt who drank the river dry.
But, no, you're alive, heaving I'll bet,
against the head of someone's bed.
I can almost catch your scent, my sweet,
filling the dark with your luscious heat.

Familiar

I could swear I remember this bird,
one-legged on the watery sand.
Maybe because it looks like
he remembers me. I step
toward him, and instead of the usual
cavalier amble out of range,
he stays put and regards me with
a kind of pity. Eyes crossed, chest out,
the yellow-beaked flyboy looks like he's
thinking of old song titles, "Alone Again,
(Naturally)." I want to rush him like a kid,
want all of a sudden to kick him into a feathery piñata.
But there's all those guys on the stacked summer porches
drinking Molson Dry and Labatt Blue tallboys as they watch
their girlfriends brush grains of sand off their burnt bellies.

Interrogative

Did you hear what I was playing, Lane?
Will I find myself in a country garden
greeted by a girl like a pink rose?
Will her name be Cecily?
Will that crosslit garden on a wooden stage
hold my only portion of unvarnished joy?

Access

For Leah Xue

There's a sensuality I find difficult to access.
It's like finding my way around a hospital
with its five linked buildings and seventeen levels
and eighty-eight elevators and corridors beyond
count. I think it might be in neurology, but an
old friend says it's more likely in psychiatric
gerontology. Wheelchairs roll by, and strolling,
shining doctors young as gods, for whom all
is accessible. In the Brain Fit Club, the women
are beautiful and wear fetching outfits
except for the receptionist who, like a lot of old
bats, looks mean as a least weasel, but says to
me as I wait for a printout, "Glad they decided
against the Olympics?" "Yes." "I would've
left town." "I think a lot of us would," I say,
adding, "There's a sensuality I find difficult
to access." She looks up. "Tell me about it."

Raptor

I woke at three feeling heartless,
not in the sense of cruel, but in a more literal sense—
I felt my heart was missing. Not in a literal sense, really,
more in a metaphorical sense—as if my chest were raked
clean. In the kitchen, I got a glass of water and raised
the blinds and you'll never guess what I saw.
I saw you. You were a crow. It looked like a crow,
it might've been some kind of raptor. It was
a variously blue night, lots of blues, more like
dusk than three in the morning.
You were rising through the gradations
of blue. Even though it was a crow
or possibly some kind of raptor, I could tell it was you.
In its claws was a heart.
I watched it fly—watched you fly—swoop, really,
off with a single cry.

Last Evening

Last evening over summer
drinks in my old friend's kitchen, just
before dusk, I met his son's girl. Now,

he'd been talking about this young
woman as if she were his own rare pearl
not his college boy's first amour.
By his lights she could do no wrong.

But to do him justice,
he was never salacious in his praise,
"Lovely, funny, kind, frank," nothing to raise
that particular eyebrow. He kind of fussed

over her like a doting grandma.
Sent me pictures of the couple by email.
And indeed, she is a dark-eyed, dark-haired
beauty, I could see, but as my own dad

would say, pretty girls are a dime a dozen.
Then, last night, we dropped by for summer
drinks, and met in person this perfect wonder.
And she had a frank handshake, no question

about that. And her black eyes buzzed like black bees
when she laughed, and when she glanced at me
out of the corner of one, stronger than a memory
came a yearning so pure I thought I might fall.

V

Like Swallows Singing

Saccharine's what they call
him now, "ho-hum, dum dee dum."
There's surely not a lot
of folks, not even some,
I'd guess, who pull him from
the shelf, blow off the dust
and read his "anodyne" poems.
Back in the day he was a must,
rhythm's constant, rhyme's pride,
felicity's fellow; his village smithy
gave me shivers and Revere's ride
by the gleam of the tower's belfry
galloped through my young boy's head.
And even now, with you a year gone,
I return to the jingling old bard.
Still on the lookout for the bright morn
in the darkest dawn of his long life,
the optimist steps up to bat,
pulling his rabbit, sails, and swallows,
streaming lilies from his teeming hat.
His Frances was a living prayer
whose absence pierced him like an arrow,
yet he kept her silent and apart
on his anniversary of the heart.

Rain Dove

Also known as mourning dove
for its muted, round croon,
one of our most bountiful birds.
Pale feathered, slender, sometimes
spotted, it was your favorite.
And when you were a girl,
your favorite aunt,
a doggedly cheerful sort,
teased and teased, saying, "You
would love that sad old singer!"
Well, your mother was gone
and so I guess you would.
When the rain dove takes flight
its wings sing a different song,
a whirring kind of song.

Echolocation

To see old Mahlon rowing across Chain of Ponds
his boat spilling over with weightless strips
of fuchsia Styrofoam for one of the new cabins,
startling the foraging bats flitting in the dusk
who had never heard such a color before,
we fretted that the new hue was some sort
of harbinger, a portent of some quiet incursion,
but maybe we were a mite previous seeing
signs of the end everywhere, the coming
of the dreaded *autres* but didn't know (how
could we) as we rowed and waved in the
wild's low silence toward our own small
cabin with its kerosene lamps and outhouse,
that not the wilderness but you were soon
to be among the missing, you were going?
How could we know that, as you helped guide
me through the two rounded boulders marking
our landing spot and I pulled gently on one oar
and then the other to get us safely to shore?

Missing

The caregivers come and go
but you remain,
appearing at my study door
again and again
with your child's pink smile
as you forget why you're here.
"Just to while away the time," I venture,
patting the couch beside me.
You sit as I work until
the TV draws you back out.
You watch standing up now.
Sometimes I come into a
room and see you standing
for minutes at a time.

Self Help

About halfway through
your dying, you came up
with theories of your own.
It was around the time
you found an old purse:
Recipes, receipts, lint,
and observed
"This is when I was a person."

Spilling coffee again, you wondered,
"Why can't they go in and get rid
of the bodies in my brain."
Then you had some suggestions of your own.

"Maybe if I go on a swing. That might help.
A swing, like in a playground? Yes, all that
swinging, you know, might help?"
"We can do that," I say. And we can.
Seventy-eight years old, a hundred forty pounds.
I guess we can do that.

"Or if I stand on my head?"
"Not sure about that, dear,
maybe touch your toes instead."

Lie Back in My Arms

Lie back in my arms.
Let your wasted bones
melt into me like butter
into batter,
batter the color
of the crusty corners
of your always-open
mouth.
Let me relish
your stale muddy
breath as your
cabled limbs sink
into my flesh
until I've absorbed
you completely.
Long ago, my dear
you'd sit above me
holding yourself up
with young muscles,
shifting forward and back,
your breasts breaking
like easy waves
under a dawn sky.

After the Funeral

After the funeral,
after the reception,
I almost started to hurry home
to tell you all about both,
and about your death:

How in the Home, you
were, as they say, surrounded
at the end by loved ones,
meaning me and Theresa
and Judi. But as well
by the aides and nurses
who'd looked after you for two years—
how they hovered over you!
weeping like Giotto's putti.

And at the burial (and of course
I forgive them for this),
most speakers were at pains
to say you weren't gone but
transmuted—into sunlight,
the song of birds, the sound of rain,
a thread in the web of the cosmos.
Or that you were in Paradise
reunited with the mother
you lost at twelve. "She's not gone," they
said, "She's not gone but altered"
When I got home, all the rooms
in the house were empty.

We Were Sitting by the River

We were sitting by the river on a green wooden bench
as the light subsided slowly and the coxswains'
urgent voices faded underneath the footbridge where
I grew up. I'd caught a fish nearby with my bare hands
when I was eight and carried it flipping across the highway,
placing it carefully in one of our garbage cans that I filled
with a few feet of water. Mom lost her temper when
she nosed the fish a few days later. I laughed at the look
on her wide floury face and a moment later she laughed too.

We were sitting by the river on a green wooden bench
as the light subsided slowly and the coxswains'
urgent calls faded around a bend in the swift flow.
I turned to say something to you and you were gone.

Insomnia

Stars, some dead, quiver
on the pane.
Bourbon and Scotch,
never go bad.

Time qua time,
says the physicist,
is an illusion; yet the ice deliquesces,
stars blench in the appalling sky.

Keeping Busy

Someone's working outside somewhere,
a small machine, a hand-held sander,
maybe. The sound follows me
from window to open window.
I'm on a quest, a picture hanging
from one finger of each hand, intent
on my small chore, on some requited
kind of feeling when I find the right place
for the right painting, the right measure
of space and light—where it can reside
in its own brightness, its own mood.
A leafy village scene, canting steeple,
rippling stream; a sepia couple embracing,
naked and floating in their small frame.
Maybe near the fading Parrish you loved so shyly:
the pensive young girl by a blurry sea,
her arms 'round her knees, her eyes half-closed.

About the Author

Alec Solomita is a writer and artist working in the Boston area. His fiction has appeared in the *Southwest Review, The Mississippi Review, Southword Journal,* and *Peacock,* among other publications. He was shortlisted by the Bridport Prize and *Southword Journal.* His poetry has appeared in *Poetica, Lothlorien Poetry Journal, Litbreak, Driftwood Press, Anti-Heroin Chic, The Galway Review, The Lake,* and elsewhere, including several anthologies. His photographs and drawings can be found in *Fatal Flaw, Young Ravens Review, Tell-Tale Inklings,* and other publications. He took the cover photo and designed the cover of his poetry chapbook, "Do Not Forsake Me," which was published in 2017.

〰

www.ingramcontent.com/pod-product-compliance
Lightning Source LLC
Chambersburg PA
CBHW020228090426
42735CB00010B/1622